MW00397552

# ABOUT MISS WAH

GRAPHIC DESIGNER & SPONSORED STREET ARTIST KNOWN AS 'MISS WAH'
LIVES IN WORCESTERSHIRE, ENGLAND SURROUNDED BY SKETCHBOOKS,
MARKERS AND SPRAY PAINT!

SHE BEGAN HER LOVE OF DOODLING FROM A VERY YOUNG AGE
DRAWING ON ANYTHING SHE COULD GET HER HANDS ON
INCLUDING SEVERAL IMPORTANT LETTERS FROM THE BANK PLUS COUNTLESS
MAGAZINE COVERS (BECAUSE MODELS MAKE GREAT PIRATES... OBVIOUSLY!)
NOW IN HER THIRTIES NOTHING HAS REALLY CHANGED!

AFTER STARTING A SUCCESSFUL YOUTUBE CHANNEL - SHE BEGAN TO REALISE A LOT OF
PEOPLE SHARED HER LOVE FOR HER CUTE CHARACTERS.
SHE BEGAN TO CREATE MORE AND MORE CANVASES, STICKERS AND WHEAT PASTES,
IN TURN PROGRESSING ONTO MARKER MURALS AND SPRAY PAINT PIECES AROUND THE
WORLD. THESE PIECES GAINED HER SPONSORSHIP FROM UNI POSCA.

SHE NOW RUNS HER OWN BUSINESS AND SPENDS ALL OF HER FREE TIME CREATING
COMMISSIONS, DRINKING A LOT OF TEA, EDITING VIDEOS, READING FAR TOO MANY BOOKS,
AND SPENDING FAR TOO MUCH TIME ON INSTAGRAM.

ISBN 978-1516928408

Copyright © Sarah Gasby 2015

The right of Sarah Gasby to be identified as the author and illustrator of this
work has been asserted by her in accordance with the Copyright, Designs and
Patents Act 1988.

All rights reserved. No part of this publication may be
reproduced, stored in a retrieval system, or transmitted, in any form,
or by any means (electronic, mechanical, photocopying,
recording or otherwise) without the prior written permission of the publisher.

# SHADES OF KAWAII
## A CUTE COLOURING BOOK

~∞ MISS WAH ∞~

WWW.MISSWAH.COM

# HUGE AMOUNT OF LOVE!

DEDICATED TO:
MY WONDERFUL PARENTS FOR ALWAYS ENCOURAGING
ME TO FOLLOW MY DREAMS & NEVER GIVE UP...
'LOVE YOU MORE!'

PAUL AKA 'MY DOG SIGHS' FOR BEING THE MOST
AMAZING FRIEND! YOUR GUIDANCE, SUPPORT & INSPIRATION
HELPED ME CREATE THIS BOOK - THANK YOU!

AND TO LORNA (YOU WERE THERE FROM DAY ONE!),
KORP, JO P, NINA, HARVEY & OLLIE
FOR YOUR CONSTANT LOVE & SUPPORT

# I WOULD LOVE TO SEE YOUR CREATIONS!

TAG A PHOTO OF YOUR FINISHED PAGES ON INSTAGRAM
@LIL_WAH - #MISSWAH #SHADESOFKAWAII
OR POST TO MY FACEBOOK PAGE
FACEBOOK.COM/LITTLEMISSWAH

## FOLLOW MISS WAH!

TWITTER: @MISSWAHOFFICIAL
YOUTUBE.COM/MISSWAH
PINTEREST.COM/LITTLEMISSWAH
INSTAGRAM: LIL_WAH
FACEBOOK.COM/LITTLEMISSWAH

WWW.MISSWAH.COM

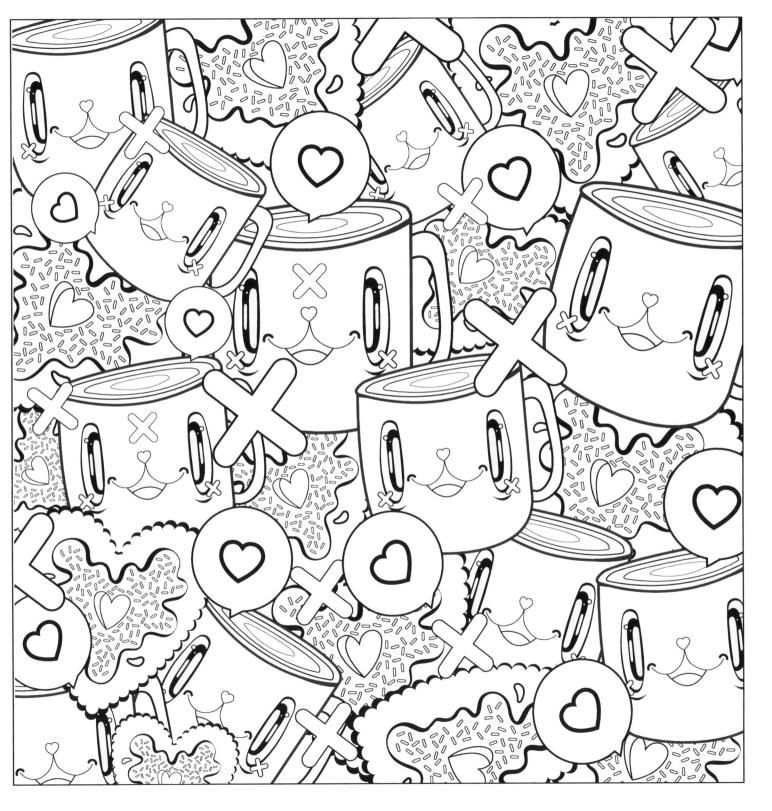

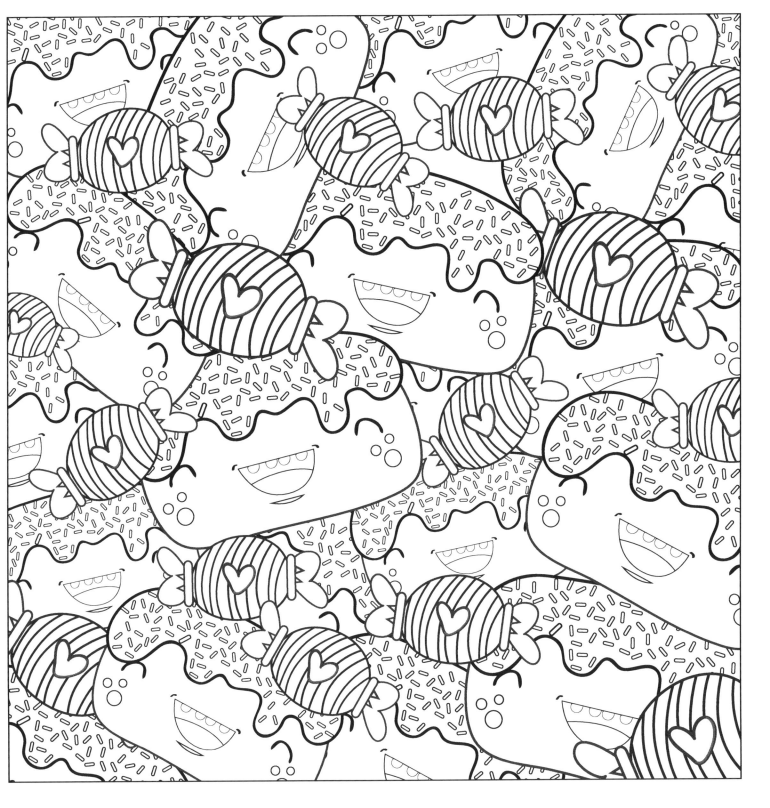

I WOULD LIKE TO SAY A BIG THANK YOU
TO EVERYONE WHO
PURCHASED 'SHADES OF KAWAII'
X

WWW.MISSWAH.COM

52189116R00031

Made in the USA
Lexington, KY
10 September 2019